For David, Angus, Joanna, Robert and Icilda —
five very special gifts

THE GIFT OF
A CHILD

Written and compiled by Marion Stroud

1817

HARPER & ROW, PUBLISHERS, SAN FRANCISCO

Cambridge, Hagerstown, New York, Philadelphia,
London, Mexico City, São Paulo, Sydney

Acknowledgements
The photographs in this book are reproduced by permission of the following photographers and organizations:
Colour Library International: 'Step of faith', 'The real me'.
Lion Publishing/David Alexander: 'Today', 'Tomorrow's memories' (children on boat, both photographs on right-hand page).
Pictor International: 'Child care', 'Forgive me', 'Energy gap',
'Reason to believe', 'A prayer for fathers', 'Thank you', 'Love is . . .' and cover photograph.
All remaining photographs by Lion Publishing/Jon Willcocks.

Bible quotations as follows: Psalm 127:3 and Mark 10:14,16 ('Your link with life'), Proverbs 22:6 and 29:15,17a ('Love means discipline'), Deuteronomy 6:4-7,20-21a and Proverbs 3:1, 5-7,11-12 ('Reason to believe') from *Good News Bible*, copyright 1966, 1971 and 1976 American Bible Society, published by Bible Societies/Collins; Luke 12:22-23, 30-31 ('Setting goals') from *Holy Bible, New International Version*, copyright 1978 New York International Bible Society.

Other copyright material as follows: Extracts by Paula D'Arcy ('Perfect you' and 'So much to learn') from *Song for Sarah* © 1979 Paula D'Arcy, Harold Shaw Publishers 1979, Lion Publishing 1981; 'For all these smallnesses' from *Sitting by My Laughing Fire* © 1977 Ruth Bell Graham, Word Books, Publisher, Texas 1977; 'Ten child care commandments' from *The Needs of Children* by Mia Kellmer Pringle, Schocken Books Inc., Hutchinson 1980; 'I was so cross to the children' from *I've got to talk to somebody, God* © 1968, 1969 by Marjorie Holmes Mighell, reprinted by permission of Hodder and Stoughton Ltd and Doubleday and Company, Inc; 'Companions to our children' and 'Don't tell me' from *For the love of children* © 1979 Ulrich Schaffer, Lion Publishing 1980; 'Children take time' from *How do you find the time?* by Pat King, Tyndale House Publishers 1975, Pickering & Inglis 1982; 'A prayer for fathers' from *Who am I, God?* © 1970, 1971 by Marjorie Holmes Mighell, reprinted by permission of Hodder and Stoughton Ltd and Doubleday and Company, Inc.

Every effort has been made to trace and contact copyright owners. If there are any inadvertent omissions in the acknowledgements, we apologize to those concerned.

Printed in Italy by New Interlitho S.P.A., Milan.

Library of Congress Cataloging in Publication Data

Stroud, Marion.
    The Gift of a Child.

    1. Children—Miscellanea.   2. Infants—Miscellanea.   I. Title.

HQ767.9.S79 1983   305.2'3   82-48937

ISBN 0-06-067755-4

83 84 85 86 87   10 9 8 7 6 5 4 3 2 1

A new person has come
to share the freedom and the flowers
and the heartache and the hope
with those of us
who already know them.

Herb and Mary Montgomery

YOUR LINK WITH LIFE

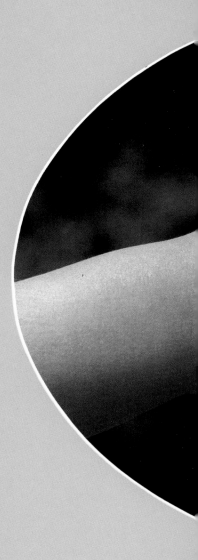

Children are a gift from the Lord;
they are a real blessing.

The Book of Psalms

Jesus... said to his disciples, 'Let the children
come to me, and do not stop them, because the
Kingdom of God belongs to such as these...'
Then he took the children in his arms, placed his
hands on each of them, and blessed them.

Mark's Gospel

Mankind owes to the child
the best it has to give.

United Nations Declaration

Before I got married I had six theories about
bringing up children; now I have six children
and no theories.

John Wilmot, Earl of Rochester (1647-80)

A mother clasping her little girl's hand, a father
gripping the fingers of his small son — each is
leading his own dreams forward, holding fast to
his own tomorrows... A child's hand in
yours... is your link with life itself.

Marjorie Holmes

PERFECT YOU

You're Sarah!. . . First we're laughing, then we're crying. We can't believe it. . . The end was so fast — you insistent, me scared. And your daddy tripping to get into his delivery room 'whites'. And then you. Ten fingers, ten toes, little you. Perfect you.

Watching you stretch your way into this world was the fullest joy I've ever known. Complete. No happiness in my life has ever been that true. I'll carry your first cry with me everywhere I go. . .

Paula D'Arcy

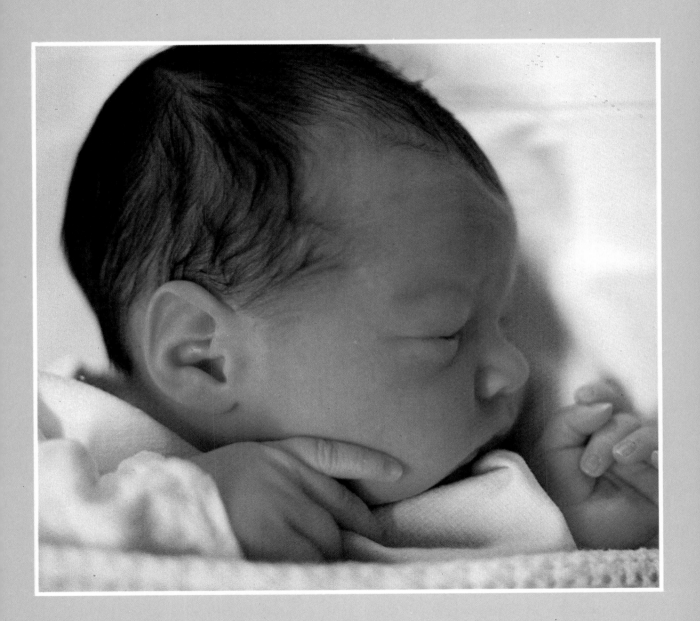

SO MUCH TO LEARN

Dear Sarah:
What's happening? Why are you crying? And why can't I figure out why you're crying? I thought I was as cool and capable as they came. But look at me. Who'd have guessed being a parent wasn't easy?. . . What an adjustment from merely being someone's daughter to also being someone's (your!) mother. It's overwhelming that you depend so totally on me.

In the hospital motherhood all seemed adventurous and exciting. But here at home I'm way too tired to be poetic. Some days it's a contest to see who cries more, you or I. How lucky we are that your daddy is so uncomplaining.

Dear Sarah, do you think we'll make it?

Dear Sarah:
Was I the one who secretly doubted that one little baby could significantly change our lives? . . . I had a lot to learn! We are indeed very different with you! The days that were ours have all become yours. You first. . .

Did I often make it hard for you, those first months? There I was trying to soothe you with one arm, furiously turning the pages of my Dr. Spock with the other. I really apologize for being so new and shaky!. . . It seems so much better now. I mean, I'm far from a pro, but I do think I'm getting used to us. . .

Your daddy wrote a poem about us which says that we three are like a strong tree with good roots. One of us alone would be buffeted by the wind. But together we're strong.

You two nourish me with your love.

Paula D'Arcy

NIGHT-WATCH

'People who say they sleep like a baby usually don't have one!'

Why is it, Lord God, that he seldom wants to sleep when we do? This child — he's like a human whirlwind in the daytime, and still wakes up at three in the morning to play. If he were ill or cold or hungry we could soothe him, but he's just bored, a little lonely, wide-awake.

We've tried the remedies that they've suggested. We've put toys into his cot, a night-light in his room, fed him, watered him, picked him up, left him to cry. . . and still we keep night-watch while all around is wrapped in blissful, peaceful sleep.

We need your help, dear God. Help us to be grateful for his glowing health, boundless energy and seemingly endless curiosity. Give us the strength we need to face each new morning; clear thinking for the day's work; patience with the little problems that loom so large when we are tired, and wisdom so that we may know just how to meet his needs. And most of all help us to hang on to the assurance that, as with all of childhood's phases, this too will pass, and one night we'll all enjoy some quiet, unbroken sleep.

SMALL IS BEAUTIFUL

For all these smallnesses
I thank You, Lord:

small children
and small needs;
small meals to cook,
small talk to heed,
and a small book
from which to read
small stories;
small hurts to heal,
small disappointments, too,
as real
as ours;
small glories
to discover
in bugs,
pebbles,
flowers.

When day is through
my mind is small,
my strength is gone;
and as I gather
each dear one
I pray, 'Bless each
for Jesus' sake —
such angels sleeping,
imps awake!'

What wears me out
are little things:
angels minus
shining wings.
Forgive me, Lord,
if I have whined;
. . . it takes so much
to keep them shined;
yet each small rub
has its reward,
for they have blessed me.

Thank you,
Lord.

Ruth Bell Graham

TODAY

Today you ran circles around the average athlete in training
    scaled more impossible climbs than
        the average mountaineer
    talked faster and for longer than the average disc jockey
    asked more questions than the average
        quizmaster on a busy day
    and untidied the entire house faster than a force 8 gale.

Today you were three years old.

Today I walked one mile and ran at least two
    performed three emergency rescues and four
        minor operations
    answered questions on natural history, mechanics,
        astronomy and religion
    acted as nursemaid, chauffeur, housekeeper,
        cook and free-lance entertainer.

Today I was your mother.

CHILD CARE

'Ten Commandments'

1

Give continuous, consistent, loving care — it's
as essential for the mind's health as food is for
the body.

2

Give generously of your time and
understanding — playing with and reading to
your child matters more than a tidy,
smooth-running home.

3

Provide new experiences and bathe your child in
language from birth onwards — they enrich his
growing mind.

4

Encourage him to play in every way both by
himself and with other children — exploring,
imitating, constructing, pretending and creating.

5

Give more praise for effort than for
achievement.

6

Give him ever-increasing responsibility — like
all skills, it needs to be practised.

7

Remember that every child is unique — so
suitable handling for one may not be right
for another.

8

Make the way you show disapproval fit your
child's temperament, age and understanding.

9

Never threaten that you will stop loving him or
give him away; you may reject his behavior
but never suggest that you might reject him.

10

Don't expect gratitude; your child did not ask to
be born — the choice was yours.

Mia Kellmer Pringle

FORGIVE ME

Oh, God, I was so cross to the children today. Forgive me.

Oh, God, I was so discouraged, so tired, and so unreasonable. I took it out on them. Forgive me.

Forgive me my bad temper, my impatience, and most of all my yelling. I cringe to think of it. My heart aches. I want to go down on my knees beside each little bed and wake them up and beg them to forgive me. Only I can't, it would only upset them more.

I've got to go on living with the memory of this day. My unjust tirades. The guilty fear in their eyes as they flew about trying to appease me. Thinking it all their fault — my troubles, my disappointments.

Dear God, the utter helplessness of children. Their vulnerability before this awful thing, adult power. And how forgiving they are, hugging me so fervently at bedtime, kissing me goodnight. And all I can do now is to straighten a cover, move a toy fallen out of an upthrust hand, touch a small head burrowed into a pillow, and beg in my heart, 'Forgive me'.

Lord, in failing these little ones whom you've put into my keeping, I'm failing you. Please let your infinite patience and goodness fill me tomorrow. Stand by me, keep your hand on my shoulder. Don't let me be so cross to my children.

Marjorie Holmes

ENERGY GAP

Dear Lord God, are all six-year-old boys like this — a bundle of noisy, tumbling, talking humanity who is on the move from the moment that he erupts out of bed in the morning until he collapses between the covers at night — unless there are cartoons on television! He has the appetite of a horse, the arguing ability of a barrack-room lawyer, the curiosity of a cat and the lung power of a sergeant-major! He is too big to be babied, but too small to be given much responsibility.

Sometimes, God, he doesn't seem to know how to cope with all that life and energy pent up inside one small body, and since he's as fearless as he's fidgety, he must work his guardian angel overtime! Help him, God. And please help us. Help us to find ways for him to channel his energy; to stretch that developing body and mind in safety. Thank you for school, for gym clubs and swimming pools. Thank you for libraries, for parks and museums and all the things that we can do and discover in our own back garden. Thank you for all the fun he finds in each day. Please help us to enjoy him as he is now — and enable us all to savor the great adventure of being six years old, together.

LOVE MEANS DISCIPLINE

Teach a child how he should live,
and he will remember it all his life.
The Book of Proverbs

The child who has everything done for him, everything given to
him, and nothing required of him is a deprived child. . . The
parent who tries to please the child by giving in to him and
expecting nothing from him ends up by pleasing no one, least of
all the child. For in the end, when trouble results, the child will
blame the parent for his gutlessness.
Larry Christenson

Discipline is demanded of the athlete to win a game. Discipline is
required for the captain running his ship. Discipline is needed for
the pianist to practise for the concert. Only in the matter of
personal conduct is the need for discipline questioned. But if
parents believe standards are necessary, then discipline certainly
is needed to attain them.
Gladys Brooks

Correction and discipline are good for children. If a child has his
own way, he will make his mother ashamed of him. . . Discipline
your son and you can always be proud of him.
The Book of Proverbs

COMPANIONS

Lord,
sometimes I am frightened by the weight I feel
to bring up these children
that you have entrusted to me
because in our time,
full of confusion and potential,
it seems harder and harder
to know how to raise children.

I know that I will make mistakes,
that I will fail my children,
that my strength and patience will not be sufficient,
that I will make the wrong decisions,
and that at times my love will grow weak.

Around me I see parents
laboring under the same weight,
afraid in the same way,
trying their best,
reading, feeling, growing
to stay close to their children
so that they will have the best possible start.

Help us all to keep love going,
and put your blessing on our love
which then has a chance to overcome
all the mistakes we will make.
Help us to know what it means practically
to be real companions to our children.

Ulrich Schaffer

LEARNING FOR LIFE

If a child lives with criticism
He learns to condemn.

If a child lives with hostility
He learns to fight.

If a child lives with ridicule
He learns to be shy.

If a child lives with shame
He learns to feel guilty.

If a child lives with tolerance
He learns to be patient.

If a child lives with encouragement
He learns confidence.

If a child lives with praise
He learns to appreciate.

If a child lives with fairness
He learns justice.

If a child lives with security
He learns to have faith.

If a child lives with approval
He learns to like himself.

If a child lives with acceptance and friendship
He learns to find love in the world.

Dorothy Law Nolte

REASON TO BELIEVE

Many parents do nothing about their children's religious education, telling them they can decide what they believe when they're twenty-one. That's like telling them they can decide when they're twenty-one, whether or not they should brush their teeth. By then, their teeth may have fallen out. Likewise, their principles and morality may also be non-existent.

Princess Grace of Monaco

Remember this! The Lord — and the Lord alone — is our God. Love the Lord your God with all your heart, with all your soul, and with all your strength. Never forget these commands that I am giving you today. Teach them to your children. . . In time to come your children will ask you, 'Why did the Lord our God command us to obey all these laws?' Then tell them. . .

The Book of Deuteronomy

Don't forget what I teach you, my son. Always remember what I tell you to do. . . Trust in the Lord with all your heart. Never rely on what you think you know. Remember the Lord in everything you do, and he will show you the right way. Never let yourself think that you are wiser than you are; simply obey the Lord and refuse to do wrong. . . When the Lord corrects you, my son, pay close attention and take it as a warning. The Lord corrects those he loves, as a father corrects a son of whom he is proud.

The Book of Proverbs

STEP OF FAITH

'You tell me all this about God', he said, five years old and already a sceptic, 'but how can I know that you're right? What if there are other gods. . . how will I know which one is true?'

'Other gods'? Yes, there will be many other gods that will demand your worship. Invisible gods. Love of material things; lust for power; single-minded pursuit of selfish ambition and the other so-called 'good things' of life. And the more visible gods of other faiths and other cultures which will tempt you with offers of peace and happiness. So how *can* you know. . . and what should we teach you, when we too have our questions, our fears and our failings?

We can teach you only what we ourselves have found to be true, those things on which we have built our lives. We can make you aware of an all-knowing, all-powerful, all-loving, heavenly Father, who cares about you as an individual and has promised to be found by everyone who truly seeks him. We can teach you the facts and we must live out their implications. But the final step of faith is yours to take — alone.

TAKE TIME

Don't tell me
how much you love me;
show me by having time for me.

Ulrich Schaffer

Children take time. Therein lies the problem. . . children take so much time.

It takes half an hour to feed a toddler breakfast.
Half an hour to bathe and dress him.
Half an hour to clean up what he shouldn't have gotten into.
It takes half an hour to sit with a four-year-old working a puzzle for the first time.
It takes half an hour to listen to a six-year-old's reading lesson.
It takes half an hour to coach a teenager in history.
It takes twenty minutes to share a cup of camomile tea with a young daughter.
It takes fifteen minutes, six times a day, to discipline a child who had decided to test you.
It takes fifteen minutes each night to listen to each child's prayer.

It's easy to see why we may have a problem. All these things that must be done with our children are at war with all that society tells us or that we tell ourselves we must do elsewhere. . .

For me the war ended abruptly with the realization that I didn't have to be any of those people that magazines so subtly insisted I should be. I didn't have to be a great housekeeper or an enviable cook. . . I didn't have to be any of the women that the school and the media insisted were so important: the politically involved, the champion of the downtrodden or even the exciting, innovative hostess.

If we have been called by God to be mothers, let's drop all the activities that are making it so painful for us to enjoy our children. For everyone who says, 'But society needs me. I can't sit back and not do my share', I would say, 'Let's give our children the time they need to help them grow into secure people'. We are adding a greater burden to society than we could ever compensate for with all our good deeds if we don't spend time training our children, time helping them to be secure as people.

Pat King

CHILD'S-EYE VIEW

'I sometimes wish', he sighed, as I whirled into
the bedroom to kiss him goodnight, 'that you
could be a quiet, country mother, and just sit
and knit! But I suppose it's against your nature!'

'I want to be one like Mom when I grow up,'
she told them.
     'What kind of a one is that?' I asked,
overhearing, thinking of my profession, my
committees, my hobbies and interests.
     'You know', she answered, 'one who cooks
and cleans and kisses you better!'

'John's mother goes out to work now,' he
told me.
     'Would you like it if I had a job?'
I asked him.
     'I wouldn't mind', he said, considering the
matter, 'if you were a secret agent!'

It's hard to believe, dear God, that those three
children are all talking about the same woman.
How differently they see their mother and what
fun it is to be her. But Lord, most of the time it's
very hard to know if I'm making a success of the
job. Next month, next year, their needs will be
different — but will I recognize that fact? Please
give me the flexibility to grow and develop with
my children, the personal stability to help them
to feel safe and secure, and the wisdom and
insight to be the mother that they need at all
ages and stages, and still to have some part of
me left over — for my husband, and for me!

ONE OF THE FAMILY

To me you are special.
Special, because you belong to me, and are mine.
The fact that I didn't give birth to you
doesn't make me less of a mother,
or you my daughter.
For mothering is far more than birth,
and growing is something
that we can experience together,
at our own pace.
I longed for you,
though I didn't know then your face.
And when at last you were chosen,
my life took on a new dimension.
We were a family.
Now as you continue to develop,
I see mirrored in your personality
a reflection of our own ways.
And a bond has been created —
of love, warmth and security.

Claire Short

Not flesh of my flesh,
Not bone of my bone,
But still miraculously my own.
Never forget for a single minute
You didn't grow under my heart, but in it.

THE REAL ME

My mother wishes that I could be more organized and less messy — without so much 'dustable' clutter in my life — so that she would be thought to be a good housekeeper and our house an 'ideal home'.

My father wishes that I would get good marks at school, so that he could talk about me to his friends at work, and be thought a successful father.

My grandparents wish that I was younger so that I could be babied, or older, with more achievements, so that they could be proud grandparents.

My teacher wishes that I would be quiet and not ask awkward questions, so that she could be a good teacher without too much effort.

My coach wishes that I would be a good player so that his would be the winning team.

I wish that they would encourage me to do well what I *can* do. I wish that they would stop blaming me for failing to do what I have no ability to do, and allow me to branch out, experiment and explore.

I wish that they could be there when I need them, and yet set me free to discover for myself who I am, why I am here and where I am going.

I wish that I was sure that they loved me, the real me, just as I am, here and now.

SHOPPING WITH A DAUGHTER

Thank you, God, for this day that I will spend shopping with a daughter. Thank you for the fun it will be to look for pretty, fashionable things, with someone who actually *enjoys* shopping. Thank you for time to spend together. In our talking, help us to share more than comparative costs, or why 'Mary's mother would never let her wear that!'

But, Lord, you know that these outings are not always filled with sweetness and light. So please help me to allow her genuine choice; to refrain from pushing her into buying something that she doesn't like which will be a constant source of friction between us for ever after. And help her to be reasonable, Lord. To understand that our budget is limited, and that it is both unwise and unnecessary to try to look years older than she is. May we both feel, when we tramp home, footsore and (hopefully) heavy-laden, that it's been a good day. Come with us, Lord, on this day that I will spend shopping with a daughter.

SHARING SKILLS

It would be so much easier to do it myself. To avoid the grumbles, the arguments and the reminders. The calling you back to do it again . . . and again . . . and again, until it is right.

It would be so much quicker to do it my way; to avoid having to stop to show you how things work, where the tools are, what the recipe means. There would be fewer mistakes, less mess, fewer breakages and fewer squabbles about whose turn it is. But there would also be no new skills acquired for the future, no satisfaction in a job well done, and no sense of sharing, caring and being involved. For responsibility is a skill which, like any other, has to be learned.

SETTING GOALS

Jesus said. . . 'Do not worry about your life,
what you will eat; or about your body, what
you will wear. Life is more than food, and . . .
clothes . . . your Father knows that
you need them. But seek his kingdom, and
these things will be given to you as well.

Luke's Gospel

Heavenly Father, please give our children the
right goals. Keep them from drifting, from going
with the crowd to gain popularity and plenty
of friends.

Please enable them to sort out their strengths
and their weaknesses. Help them to see their
talents and abilities, not as accidents of birth or
a random combination of genes, but as gifts
from yourself, to be treasured, developed and
used in living life as you, God, mean it to be
lived. And help them to have their priorities
right. Then the rest of life's concerns will fall
into place.

It's not an easy thing we're asking for them,
Father. Life lived this way is the tough option:
blood, sweat, toil and tears. We dare not try to
influence them ourselves, for often we have
chosen the level path instead of the mountain
slopes, and because we love them so much, we
want to protect them from hurt.

But you, Lord God, know the end from the
beginning. You know why you have created
these children just the way they are,
for such a time as this. So we would ask
you Father — please give our children
the right goals.

A PRAYER FOR FATHERS

God bless fathers, all fathers old and young.

Bless the new father holding his son or daughter in his arms for the first time. (Steady his trembling, Lord, make his arms strong.) Give him the ambition and strength to provide for its physical needs. But even more, give him the love and common sense to provide for its hungering heart.

Give him the time and the will to be its friend. Give him wisdom, give him patience, give him justice in discipline.

Make him a hero in his youngster's eyes. So that the word Father will always mean a person to be respected, a fair and mighty man.

And God bless older fathers too. Fathers who are weary from working for their young. Fathers who are sometimes disappointed, discouraged. Fathers whose children don't always turn out the way they'd hoped; fathers of children who seem thoughtless, ungrateful, critical, children who rebel.

Bless those fathers, Lord; comfort them.

And stay close to all these fathers when they must tell sons and daughters goodbye. When kids leave home, going off to college, or to marry, or to war — fathers need to be steadied in their trembling then too, Lord. (Mothers aren't the only ones who cry.)

You, our Heavenly Father, must surely understand these earthly fathers well.

We so often disappoint you, rebel against you, fail to thank you, turn away from you. So, in your infinite love (and infinite experience!) bless fathers, all fathers old and young.

Marjorie Holmes

LETTING GO

Give your children up to God. . . it is utterly
safe to place your children in God's sure hands.

John White

'I'll be back', he said, 'sometime!'

And with that he left; a rebel, rejecting
education, a job — with or without prospects —
belonging; just another gesture of
nonconformity from a boy who has always
seemed compelled to be desperately and
defiantly different.

His mother would have argued, pleaded
with him, tried to persuade him to give things
one more try.

But I let him go: Lord God, I had to let him
go. For that is what you, the Father of all people,
do with us. You could have made us puppets,
but instead you gave us freedom. And I knew
that the time had come to give that to him — the
dignity of choice, and the responsibility to live
with the consequences of that choice. Be with
him in that 'far country', wherever it is. If, like
that prodigal in the Bible, he ends up starving
and destitute, remind him that our door stands
open for his return. And when that day comes,
Father, help me to welcome him back with the
same open-hearted accepting love that you
offer — to us both.

THANK YOU

Thank you, God, for this family — just for once all seated at the breakfast-table at the same time, brushed and bright-eyed, ready and eager for a new day.

Thank you that on this sparkling sunny morning no one has fought for possession of the newspaper, spilled the coffee, burnt the toast or tripped over the dog.

Thank you that the beginning of this day is not marred by fear of a test, a feud with a friend or homework mislaid.

Thank you for cheerful conversation, help given, unasked, and a kiss-in-passing from a son who long since thought himself too big for such open displays of affection.

Thank you, God, for this family. Thank you that as well as the expense, the worries and the grey Mondays, we have days like this: jewel-bright, filled with love and laughter. Help me to appreciate it now and remember it later when the storms blow up again. And today and every day — thank you, God, for this family.

HAPPY FAMILIES

There is no such thing as a 'perfect family', and happiness does not come gift-wrapped. But a truly happy family can be created when each member of that family resolves to put these principles into practice:

1 We will try not to take the little things of daily life for granted, but will show our appreciation, both by our words and actions, of clothes that are washed, meals that are cooked and financial needs that are supplied.

2 We will accept that just as the pleasures and comforts of home life are equally available to all, so are the chores and responsibilities, and we will each do our share without grumbling.

3 We will look for something to praise before we criticize, and when criticism is necessary, we will make sure that it is constructive. We will aim to build up rather than to tear down.

4 We will recognize the importance of effort as well as of achievement and praise both equally.

5 We will not offer more kindness, consideration and understanding to those outside the family than to those within it.

'Please', 'Thank you' and 'I love you' will often be said amongst us.

6 We will not demand perfection in the behavior of other family members until we can offer it to them ourselves. When we are bad-tempered or in the wrong we will admit it and apologize.

7 We will try to remember at all times that people matter more than things. This being so, we will not covet our neighbour's stereo, new car, foreign holidays, kitchen gadgets, electronic marvels, income tax rebate, promotion or anything else that is theirs. Instead we will give first place to the development of the qualities valued by God: love, joy, peace, patience, kindness, faithfulness, gentleness and self-control.

8 We will accept our home and the people in it as God's specially chosen gift to us, perfectly designed for our growth and development as individuals. We will encourage and believe in one another, accepting the need for risks, the possibility of failure, but also the potential for success if we set out prayerfully on this perilous but exciting enterprise of being a family.

TOMORROW'S MEMORIES

Each day comes just once in a lifetime — today you are creating tomorrow's memories. Invest in positive memories, for childhood memories mould the person of the future.

Last month, Dad was kept late at the office and forgot to phone and let
Mom know.
Last month, Mom was mad with him, and snapped and snarled at the rest of us.
Last month, my brother had a fight with the boy next door.
Last month, someone broke the window, and no one would own up.
Last month, Grandmother was ill, we overslept three mornings in a row, and lost one pair
of shoes and two pages of homework.
I think that last month is best forgotten, but Dad says 'No'. He says that last
month we learned *what not to do*, and that is a memory well worth keeping.

Last week, a rare snowfall transformed our world into a winter wonderland.
And we, who are so often far too pressed to play, just left the dirty dishes in the
sink, the house not tidied, weekend chores undone. Not for the sake of business
calls or family crises, but so that we could build a family of fat snow people,
lining the garden path like ghostly guards as darkness fell. And now the snow is
gone, but not the chores. Jostling with others, they demand attention still. So
were those carefree hours time lost? No, rather they were time invested — in
a memory.

LOVE IS...

Love is. . . pacing the floor through the hours
   after midnight,
   soothing your crying with love-words and lullabies,
   when all of my being is begging for rest.

Love is . . . a painting of a scarlet giant with no arms and a
   single eye, bearing that heart-stopping legend in
   wobbly letters: 'My Mommy is best'.

Love is. . . reading the same story for the sixth night
   running and not missing any of it out.

Love is. . . the last sticky sweet in the bag, only slightly
   licked and faintly dusted with dirt and dog-hairs,
   resolutely not eaten, because you had decided to keep
   it for me.

Love is. . . learning new skills so that we can help you to
   develop yours.

Love is . . . cold coffee and a soggy roll placed tenderly by
   our bed at 6.30 a.m., so that I don't have to get up
   early on my birthday.

Love is. . . caring enough to say 'no', even if 'everybody
   else is doing it'.

Love is. . . wearing a collar and tie for your cousin's
   wedding — because we asked you to.

Love is. . . letting you go with a lump in my throat, a
   prayer in my heart and a smile on my face, as you
   stride out of the door to take on the world.

Love is. . . struggling to share the faith that is our sure
   foundation, so that you, a child of the present, can
   have light for the future.